AWESOME
ARMORED
ANIMALS

ARMADILLOS

Bethany Baxter

PowerKiDS press

New York

Published in 2014 by The Rosen Publishing Group, Inc.
29 East 21st Street, New York, NY 10010

First Edition

Editor: Julia Quinlan
Book Design: Greg Tucker
Book Layout: Kate Vlachos

Photo Credits: Cover Heiko Kiera/Shutterstock.com; pp. 4, 8 Steve Bower/Shutterstock.com; p. 5 Nicholas Smythe/ Photo Researchers/Getty Images; p. 6 © iStockphoto.com/p–pix; p. 7 Brandon Seidel/Shutterstock.com; p. 9 Thierry Grun/Photographer's Choice/Getty Images; p. 10 Theo Allofs/The Image Bank/Getty Images; p. 11 Martha Marks/ Shutterstock.com; pp. 12–13 mlorenz/Shutterstock.com; pp. 14, 15, 16, 18 Bianca Lavies/National Geographic/Getty Images; p. 17 Kokhanchikov/Shutterstock.com; p. 19 Vanderlei Almeida/AFP/Getty Images; p. 20 Jeff R. Clow/Flickr/ Getty Images; p. 21 Laura Coles/E+/Getty Images; p. 22 © iStockphoto/erniedecker.

Library of Congress Cataloging-in-Publication Data

Baxter, Bethany.
 Armadillos / by Bethany Baxter. — First edition.
    pages cm. — (Awesome armored animals)
 Includes index.
 ISBN 978-1-4777-0797-5 (library binding) — ISBN 978-1-4777-0966-5 (pbk.) — ISBN 978-1-4777-0967-2 (6-pack)
 1. Armadillos—Juvenile literature. I. Title.
 QL737.E23B39 2014
 599.3'12—dc23
                              2013000197

Manufactured in the United States of America

CPSIA Compliance Information: Batch #S13PK6: For Further Information contact Rosen Publishing, New York, New York at 1-800-237-9932

Contents

Little Armored Ones

Nine-banded armadillos are the most widespread armadillo species. They live in North America, Central America, and South America.

Armadillos are **mammals** that have bodies covered in bony plates. The plates cover their heads, backs, legs, and tails. The plates form a hard shell that acts like armor. This helps keep armadillos safe from predators. In fact, "armadillo" means "little armored one" in Spanish. Armadillos are the only living mammals that have bony armored plates.

Pink fairy armadillos grow to be only between 3.5 and 4.5 inches (9–11 cm) long.

There are 20 **species** of armadillos. The giant armadillo is the largest species. It is about the size of a pig. The pink fairy armadillo is the smallest species. It is only about the size of a chipmunk! Armadillos are related to anteaters and sloths.

Warm, Western Homes

Armadillos are found only in Earth's Western **Hemisphere**. Most armadillo species are native to Central America or South America. Only the nine-banded armadillo lives in parts of North America as well.

Armadillos live in warm **habitats**. These habitats include rain forests, grasslands, marshes, and deserts. Armadillos like shady places. They also like sandy soil that is easy to **burrow** in.

Nine-banded armadillos, such as this one, like to burrow.

Hollow logs make good homes for armadillos.

Some armadillos burrow underground. Others make their homes in hollow logs. Armadillos cannot stay alive in cold weather habitats. This is because they do not have a lot of body fat to keep themselves warm.

Hard, Scaly Plates

Armadillos' plates are made of hard, scaly skin. The plates cover the tops of armadillos' bodies. Most armadillos have two large plates on their backs with smaller plates, called bands, around their middles. These bands help armadillos move more easily. Many armadillo species are named for how many bands they have.

Armadillos use their snouts to sniff around for food.

The large hairy armadillo has hair on its plates and on its underside.

For example, the three-banded armadillo has three bands, while the nine-banded armadillo has nine. Armadillos' undersides are covered in soft, hairy skin. Armadillos have shovel-shaped snouts and small eyes. They also have long claws at the ends of their toes. They use these claws for digging and burrowing.

This six-banded armadillo, also known as a yellow armadillo, is peering out of its burrow.

Armadillos are mostly solitary animals. This means they spend most of their time alone. However, in cold weather, armadillos may gather together in burrows. There, they make large nests of leaves and grass. They do this to stay warm.

Armadillos' behavior changes from season to season. This is because armadillos need to stay cool in warm weather and warm in cold weather. In warmer months, armadillos are mostly **nocturnal**. They look for insects to eat at night, when it is cooler. In colder months, armadillos become more active during the daytime. The sunlight helps keep them warm as they look for food.

The Sun is keeping this nine-banded armadillo warm as it looks for food.

Armadillo Facts!

1. The screaming hairy armadillo gets its name from the screaming noise it makes when it is scared.

2. One species of **prehistoric** armadillo, the glyptodon, was as big as a car! The glyptodon is now extinct, which means that it has died out.

3. The nine-banded armadillo can jump between 3 and 4 feet (.9m–1.2 m) into the air when it is surprised. Scientists think that this jumping action might scare off predators.

4. Armadillos have no trouble crossing lakes or rivers. They can float across the water by filling their stomachs with air. They can also sink down and walk across the bottom, holding on with their claws.

5. The Aztec people call the armadillo "azotochtli," which means "turtle-rabbit." Armadillos are said to look like rabbits under their armored plates.

6. The three-banded armadillo is the only species of armadillo that can roll up into a perfect ball to keep itself safe.

7. The giant armadillo has up to 100 teeth in its mouth! It has more teeth than any other armadillo species.

8. Armadillos evolved between 65 and 80 million years ago. They are the oldest mammal species in the Western Hemisphere.

Pups Growing Up

Male and female armadillos make babies by **mating**. Different species of armadillos mate at different times of the year. Some species mate year round.

A female armadillo gives birth between two and five months after mating. She can have a litter of one to four babies, or pups. Pups do not have hard shells when they are born.

These nine-banded armadillo pups are drinking milk from their mother.

Instead, their skin is soft and feels like leather. It hardens after a few days.

Armadillo pups drink their mothers' milk for between two and four months. Then, they switch to an adult diet. Armadillos live for between 4 and 30 years, depending on the species.

Digging for Insects

Here you can see a nine-banded armadillo's long tongue. It is perfect for catching bugs.

Armadillos are omnivores. This means that they eat both animals and plants. Their diet is made up of mostly insects and other **invertebrates**, such as worms, scorpions, and spiders. However, armadillos may also eat fruit, eggs, and small animals, such as snakes, frogs, and lizards. Some armadillos also eat carrion, or the remains of dead animals.

Armadillos use their strong sense of smell to sniff out their food. Their long claws help them dig up food if it is underground. Armadillos have peg-shaped teeth that they use to crunch the shells of insects. They also have long, sticky tongues that they use to catch insects in tunnels.

Worms are a favorite meal of armadillos.

What Eats Armadillos?

Armadillos' hard shells keep them safe from being eaten by some animals. However, armadillos still have many animal predators. Mountain lions, wolves, coyotes, jaguars, and alligators all hunt armadillos. The giant armadillo has fewer predators than smaller armadillos because of its size. Large birds sometimes swoop down and catch baby armadillos, which still have soft shells.

This startled armadillo is jumping up into the air. This reflex can scare away predators.

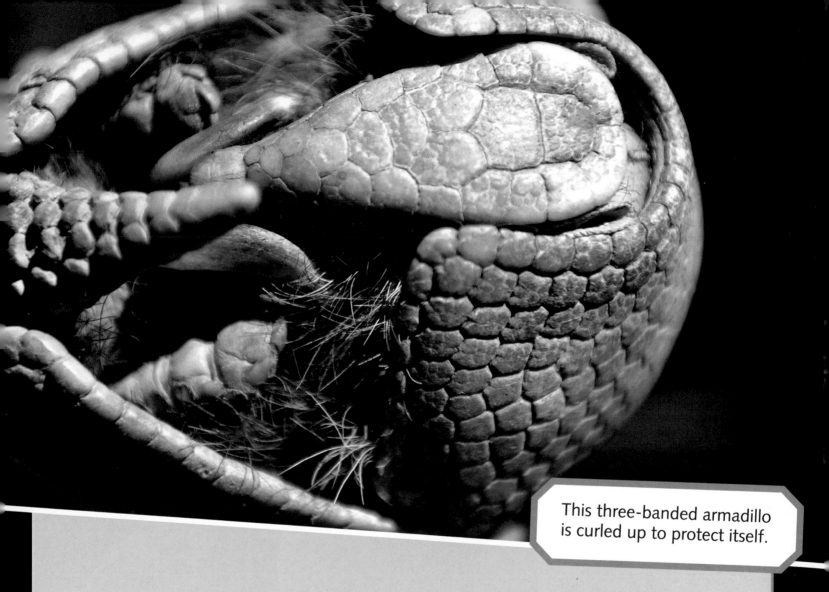

This three-banded armadillo is curled up to protect itself.

However, armadillos have many ways to **defend** themselves from animal predators. Three-banded armadillos can roll up into a tight ball so that their soft undersides are protected. Other armadillos wedge themselves in burrows, which makes it hard for predators to reach them.

Many people think of armadillos as pests. This is because armadillos are diggers and burrowers. They may make a mess in people's yards, farms, and gardens. These people sometimes call **exterminators** to get rid of armadillos near their homes.

In many places where armadillos live, the armadillo is also hunted for its meat.

Armadillos are not welcome in some places.

The **populations** of some armadillo species are getting too small because of overhunting. Smaller species of armadillos are also sometimes caught and kept as pets. Other armadillos are killed so that their scaly plates can be used for clothing and shoes. Each year, many armadillos are also killed accidentally by cars.

Humans and armadillos can get along.

Keeping Armadillos Safe

Many armadillo species are in trouble. Their numbers are getting much smaller because of overhunting. Armadillo habitats are also being destroyed in many places. Forests and grasslands are being cut down so that people can build farms and homes. **Pollution** also hurts armadillo habitats.

However, wildlife groups are working to keep armadillos from dying out. It is important to take care of Earth and its animals so that we can enjoy them for a long time to come.

Armadillos have been around for millions of years. With the help of conservation groups, they will be around for many years to come.

Glossary

burrow (BUR-oh) To dig a hole in the ground.

defend (dih-FEND) To guard from harm.

exterminators (ik-ster-mih-NAY-terz) People who get rid of pests.

habitats (HA-buh-tats) The surroundings where an animal or a plant naturally lives.

hemisphere (HEH-muh-sfeer) Half of a sphere or globe.

invertebrates (in-VER-teh-bretz) An animal without a backbone.

mammals (MA-mulz) Warm-blooded animals that have a backbone and hair, breathe air, and feed milk to their young.

mating (MAYT-ing) Joining together to make babies.

nocturnal (nok-TUR-nul) Active during the night.

pollution (puh-LOO-shun) Man-made wastes that harm Earth's air, land, or water.

populations (pop-yoo-LAY-shunz) Groups of animals or people living in the same area.

prehistoric (pree-his-TOR-ik) Having to do with the time before written history.

species (SPEE-sheez) One kind of living thing. All people are one species.

Index

Websites

Due to the changing nature of Internet links, PowerKids Press has developed an online list of websites related to the subject of this book. This site is updated regularly. Please use this link to access the list: www.powerkidslinks.com/aaa/armad/